LifeCaps Presents:

In Which Milne's Life Is Told

A Biography of Winnie the Pooh Author

A.A. Milne

By Paul Brody

◾BO͡O͡KCAPS

BookCaps™ Study Guides

www.bookcaps.com

Table of Contents

About LifeCaps

LifeCaps is an imprint of BookCaps™ Study Guides. With each book, a lesser known or sometimes forgotten life is recapped. We publish a wide array of topics (from baseball and music to literature and philosophy), so check our growing catalogue regularly (**www.bookcaps.com**) to see our newest books.

Introduction

Few authors achieve fame in their lifetime and then have that fame compound and grow long after their death. Fewer still spend much of their lives harboring resentment for the work that made them famous. Such was the case for Alan Alexander Milne. Long before he wrote *Winnie-the-Pooh*, Milne had established a career as a humorist and playwright. When his son, Christopher Robin, was born, it led to an inspiration for a series of children's verses about a toy bear named Pooh and his friends. Two novels followed that and the Winnie the Pooh brand was born.

It took Milne most of his adult life to reconcile the fact that no matter what he wrote, he had earned the label of whimsical children's author. Christopher never did seem to accept his own place in literary history, which largely amounted to lending his name to the stories. The truth is, the tales of Winnie the Pooh were about Milne's own childhood. Like many adults, he often longed for the simpler days of childhood, but unlike many adults, he had the talent to create an imaginary world that allowed him to do so. It is no coincidence that as many adults as children have been impacted by Winnie the Pooh, keeping Milne's words as much a part of modern society as they were nearly a century ago.

Chapter 1: Childhood

Perhaps it is fitting that the man whose name has become synonymous with children's fiction was raised in a world where a distinct line was drawn between the adult world and the world inhabited by children. It was the heart of the Victorian Era when Sarah "Maria" Milne gave birth to her third and final son, Alan Alexander, on January 18, 1882. Her husband, John Vince Milne, was the headmaster of Henley House, a private boarding school in London for boys aged seven through 18. Not much older than some of the senior students when he purchased Henley House in 1878, J.V. Milne grew a beard, thinking that it gave him more of an appearance of an authority figure.

Boarding schools were common in Victorian England, as was relegating the care of children to nannies and governesses. There was little concern for a child's emotional needs or development, and great care was taken to avoid "spoiling" a child. Still, J.V. wanted the school to have a family feel, and it was essential to him that the students in his care felt that they were in a loving environment. J.V. took immense satisfaction in the happiness in his pupils in an era when the vast majority of schools were not the least bit concerned if the students enjoyed their education. Education was not meant to be enjoyed. It was a process, not unlike childhood itself, that was meant to be endured as a rite of passage to adulthood.

At the age of two, young Alan began to read, pleasing his father by sounding out the word "cat," while his older brothers Barry and Ken struggled to do the same. Aland could write before he was five years old and entered kindergarten at Wykeham House. Every morning, Ken and the governess, Beatrice Edwards, walked Alan to school, where he continued to develop his reading and writing skills at a remarkable pace. Perhaps this was foreshadowing the career that was to come. As an adult, Milne would come to love *Alice in Wonderland,* but as a child, he had little interest in it. His favorite book was *Uncle Remus*, although he only wanted his father to read it out loud because J.V. was the only one who seemed to be able to read it without mangling the dialect. *Treasure Island* and *The Swiss Family Robinson* were favorites as he grew older. What he seemed to like about these stories was not the adventure but the independence of being out alone on an island. In fact, both Alan and Ken shared the fantasy about being the only two people left on Earth, free to raid every candy shop and toy store in the world away from the watchful eyes of adults.

When Milne was six years old, he joined his brothers in classes at Henley House. He was thrilled to be with Ken, who was 16 months older. Whether Ken liked it or not at that age, the two boys were inseparable, to the point that they shared a bed. Years later, as an adult, Milne wrote that he was certain it was difficult for Ken that he was the least intelligent of the two. Ken was also, in his brother's estimation, not as handsome and not as successful. However, Milne was equally certain that Ken was more kind and said, "If you knew us both, you preferred Ken." He did not feel the same way about Barry and the two brothers would not even speak to each other in Barry's final years.

Milne's relationship with his mother was best described as detached. He did not find his mother to be particularly smart and given her overall lack of participation in raising him, Milne was not even sure that she served much purpose in his life. It was J.V. who was not only the ruler of Henley House, but also the ruler of the Milne household. True to the ideals of Victorian Era parenting, Sarah relegated herself to the background. Her primary influence in the earliest years of Milne and his older brothers was to dress them like Little Lord Fauntleroys, complete with flowing, curly locks. For Milne, cutting his hair was a much-anticipated symbolic gesture of shaking off his childhood. When the deed was done, he presented his hair to his mother in a paper bag.

Maria did try to assert some authority over Alan's education. According to J.V., she expressed some concern about how studious Alan was becoming. She believed in a common opinion of the time that young boys who were too ambitious eventually burned out and grew to be dull old men. At her request, J.V. cut back on his son's classes, but Alan became so depressed that it affected his health, so J.V. reinstated a full day of classes.

When Milne was seven, a teacher would join the faculty of Henley House that would not only become extremely influential to Milne's life and career but would become famous in his own right. H.G Wells arrived at Henley House in in 1889, six years before the publication of his science fiction novella, *The Time Machine.* Even though he was still working on his undergraduate degree at London University, Wells was hired as a science teacher. He declined the opportunity to teach scriptures because he felt it was hypocritical to teach something he did not believe in. Milne did not think much of Wells as a teacher, believing that he was too impatient, but he appreciated him as a mentor and a friend.

Wells and J.V. Milne shared a belief that education went beyond simply filling a student's head with facts and then asking the student to regurgitate those facts in an exam. Wells resisted the expectation of applying the Latin names to flowers or animals and encouraged his students to experience the natural world, not simply read about it. While Wells was at Henley House, he chaperoned any number of field trips to the zoo, museums, lectures, or cricket matches. Although Wells did not teach at Henley House for long, he would remain an influence in Milne's life for many years.

Chapter 2: Milne's Education

Westminster

What J.V. Milne could not have predicted when he sent his mathematically gifted son to Westminster School shortly after he turned 11 is that a year later, Westminster would forever eliminate any chance that Alan would follow in his father's footsteps as a scholar. J.V. could not hide his disappointment at the headmaster's report in the summer of 1894 that his son has performed poorly in math and seemed to lack in ambition. Never mind the fact that the evaluation had been written before Milne had taken the math exams, which placed him the highest in his grade. The only three students who had done better were 16 through 18 years old. Still, J.V., a headmaster himself, could focus only on what the headmaster wrote.

As disappointed as J.V. was, staring at the wall rather than facing his son after reviewing the report, Milne was thrilled. It was freeing. He no longer felt that he was bound to the path of a scholar. As far as he was concerned, what did it matter? He believed without a shadow of a doubt that the report was unjust, so he was no longer going to put energy into things he did not actually want to do in the first place. Milne carried this philosophy through the rest of his life.

Westminster dates back to the 12th century and has always prided itself on a rigorous curriculum that prepares students for university academics. In Milne's era, the boarding school also believed that corporal punishment built character. Four whacks with a thick cane stung a boy's behind as well as his ego. Even if a student never faced a "tanning," the mere threat of it was terror enough. Such punishment could be issued for any number of offenses, some of which were rather vague. This sort of discipline flew in the face of how J.V. ran Henley House, but he was willing to accept it as reality for his sons in exchange for what he believed was the best possible education for them.

Even with Alan giving less than his best effort, he was still a top student at Westminster. He did learn some shortcuts along the way, though. The policy of having the students grade each other's papers rather than their own was supposed to cut down on cheating. The reality is that only encouraged more dishonesty. When an assignment had been graded, the teacher would ask what the score was on the paper he graded. The students would simply report a higher score, knowing the other students would do the same. Milne said that he certainly was not going to be the one to suggest that the boy in the desk next to him may have inflated his grade.

Ken was also at Westminster and he and Alan devised a way to pass the time in math class without the teacher realizing what they were doing. The boys would write letters to each other under the guise of doing schoolwork. Apparently the teacher was not looking at the paper closely enough to realize that they were writing about their plans for the holidays or their next cycling excursion. The boys were avid cyclers and once made a 100-mile trip in one day. None of this negatively impacted their work as they earned some of the top grades in the class.

Alan also blossomed into a good athlete at Westminster. His sports of choice were cricket and soccer. As an adult, he would be an avid golfer. However, Milne was far from an obsessed jock and unlike many at the school, was unfazed by those who had little use for sports. Ken and Alan shared their love of cricket for the rest of their lives and in his later years, few things gave Alan such pleasure as watching a good cricket match. Unfortunately for his son, he was never quite as good at the sport as Milne hoped he would be.

Westminster did little to train Milne for his career as a writer. There was not much expected of the students in the way of writing essays and certainly no creative writing. As Milne approached his 18th birthday and the end of his time at Westminster, a copy of *Granta*, the undergraduate literary magazine of the University of Cambridge, caught his eye. It reminded him of *Punch*, which all of the Milnes enjoyed. *Punch* was a weekly satirical humor magazine that had been in publication since 1841. He made it his goal to go to Cambridge and edit *Granta*. A small scholarship to help offset the costs made that possible.

Cambridge

With a scholarship in mathematics, Milne enrolled in Cambridge for the fall term in 1900. However, *Granta* was his real reason for being there and he began submitting poems to the magazine as soon as he arrived. His work first appeared in print in his second term when *Granta* published "Sonnets of Love (And Other Things)" on February 4, 1901. The poem was credited to A.K.M., which stood for Alan and Ken Milne. The brothers collaborated for two years until Ken decided that he wanted to write his own work. Typically of Ken, he initially explained his decision as one that was best for his brother because Alan could do fine without him. Hadn't Alan been doing the bulk of the work, anyway? Alan was terribly upset by this because it was far from the truth, and it was only with some pressing that Ken admitted that he wanted to work solo. It would take some time before Milne would realize that any rivalry with his brother was invented only in his head. Ken felt no such rivalry and truly only wished for the best for his younger brother.

R.C. Lehmann was the founder of *Granta* and one of the major contributors to *Punch* when he wrote Milne to congratulate him on a serial that he had written for the Cambridge magazine. Milne was not nearly as impressed with his own work as Lehmann was but was flattered at the compliment. He was likely grateful that he was even writing at all at this point. He had achieved his goal of becoming the editor of the magazine, despite the threat from the school to revoke his scholarship. He had been reminded that he was under scholarship as a math scholar, not a writer. Defiantly, Milne said that he give up the scholarship before he gave up the chance to edit *Granta*. He ultimately agreed to submit a schedule of his activities, verifying that he was spending at least six hours per day on his studies. When he was not studying, he was writing.

He would disappoint his father again, as he did at Westminster. Milne did graduate from Cambridge with a bachelor's degree in the summer of 1903 but with only Third Class honors, just one step above the average degree. It was days before J.V. spoke to his son. When J.V. came around, he and Alan discussed his future. It was not too late for him to take the exams to become a civil servant, but it would require some cramming on history, a subject in which Milne was sorely deficient. However, it was plain for J.V. to see that this was not want his son wanted for himself. Whether Milne took the exams and failed or not is not clear. What is clear is that Milne wanted to be a writer. H.G. Wells did it and Milne believed he could, too. After an honest discussion with his father, J.V. gave his blessing and Milne moved to London to begin his career as a writer.

Chapter 3: Early Literary Career (1903 – 1925)

By the time Milne got to London in the fall of 1903, he had a little over 300 of the 1,000 pounds remaining from the money his father gave him after graduating from Cambridge. He had calculated that it might last two years, although it was gone after 16 months. He took two rooms at Temple Chambers, which provided him with breakfast and cleaning and laundry service. He ate lunch cheaply enough at a local teashop. After Ken married Maud Innes in September 1905, Milne joined his brother and sister-in-law regularly for dinner, which served the dual purposes of cutting down on expenses and allowing him to spend time with family. He got along remarkably well with Maud and in many ways she was the sister he never had.

As for where to begin his writing career, Milne had his choice of a wide variety of publications to target for his articles. Still, like many budding journalists and writers, he was forced to piece together some semblance of a living as a freelancer. He was paid for contributions to publications such as the *St. James Gazette* and *Vanity Fair,* but his primary goal was always to be published in *Punch.* He was far from the only writer with that goal. *Punch* was inundated with submissions every day and did not pay contributors exceptionally well, mostly likely because it did not have to do so. Finally, in May 1904, Milne broke into print in *Punch* with a poem called "The New Game."

Milne kept in touch with H.G. Wells, who served as his mentor during this time, and it was Wells who suggested that he write a novel based on characters he had created for a series in the *St. James Gazette*. His desperation for cash was likely part of the reason that Milne took Wells up on his suggestion and wrote *Lovers in London*, a novel about the American heroine, Amelia and her cricket-playing British beau, Teddy. It was published in March 1905, although, within 10 years, Milne would be so disgusted with the book that he bought the copyright from the publisher so that it could never be reprinted.

However, at the time, the 15 pound advance on the sales of *Lovers in London* and the fact that *Punch* began to accept his work on a more regular basis kept Milne afloat financially. Still, at 24 years old, Milne felt as if his career was not moving forward. He was getting published, but he had not found his niche. Some of his work did not even carry his byline. He had tried his hand at writing plays but got nowhere with that, either. He decided that his best option for making a name for himself and securing himself as a legitimate author was to write a novel, but not just any novel. He wanted to write the novel that people did not think twice about paying several shillings for because *everyone* was talking about it.

Milne had managed to scrape together enough money to sustain him for a few months so that he could leave London for the country and focus only on writing his breakthrough novel. With his decision made, Milne wrote a letter to R.C. Lehmann at *Punch* to let him know that he should not expect any contributions from him for a while. Milne received a prompt reply from Lehmann, asking him to wait before deciding for certain that he was leaving London. Owen Seamen, the magazine's assistant editor, asked Milne if he would meet with him. Milne agreed, and Seamen explained that the magazine's editor was retiring after 26 years. Seamen would be taking over as editor. Would Milne like to be the assistant editor? It would be a part-time position, paying 250 pounds a year, not including Milne's weekly articles. He would be paid at double his current rate for any contributions. Milne could hardly believe what he was hearing. Calm on the outside but euphoric on the inside, Milne accepted the position, and the next phase of his career – and his life – was about to begin.

Chapter 4: Milne's Life and Work at *Punch*

Henry Mayhew, a writer, and Ebenezer Landells, a wood engraver, created Punch in 1841. The idea for the magazine came from a satirical newspaper from France. The magazine nearly died an early death from lack of subscribers, but it was saved by a large annual edition, "The Almanack." *Punch* continued to limp along until 1872 when it was purchased by the printing company Bradbury and Evans. Soon after that, sales took off.

The secret to *Punch's* success was its ability to tap into the trends and feelings of the various eras of British history. The writing and the cartoons – the term cartoon is credited to *Punch* – were of high quality but far from dry and boring. Writers and artists were able to make statements with a touch of humor that was both informational and entertaining. For the first fifty years of the 20th century, *Punch* was very much aligned with the British establishment. When the country suffered through two world wars during that time, the magazine saw its role as a morale-raiser.

It was into this environment that Milne began his career when he walked into the *Punch* offices in February 1906. Right off the bat, his liberal politics clashed with the conservative politics of Seamen, his editor. It was likely this difference in opinions that kept Milne away from "The Table" for so long. Every Wednesday evening, senior staff members held their staff meetings over dinners that featured plenty of food and cigars and liberal amounts of brandy. The senior staff was friendly to Milne and always stopped in to say hello, but it would be four years before Milne was invited to carve his initials into the table that served as the centerpiece of the weekly gatherings.

By 1908, Milne's work in *Punch* was widely read to the point that he was in greater demand socially. His essays on parties, cricket, golf, and other ordinary parts of a person's day made him one of the most popular humorists at *Punch*. A lesson that he learned from H.G. Wells was not to try and look too hard for something to write about. Simply writing about what was going on around him on a daily basis provided him with material for years. In fact, Milne typically put off writing his weekly column until the last minute. It was due in the printing office on Friday afternoons at 4 p.m. and it was the rare week that he started writing it before Friday morning, not wanting to think about it too much.

Much of Milne's articles and essays featured Fieldhead, the well-appointed country home of R.C. Lehman, located near the Thames. Lehman and Milne had become friends, allowing Milne into the world of lawn tennis, boating, and socializing with the intellectual crowd. He would go there often on summer weekends, no doubt taking some inspiration for his on-going, humorous chronicles of the fictional British twenty-somethings he called the Rabbits. *Punch* readers came to anticipate the stories of the young Rabbits, with Milne usually dropping in on their lives on weekends while they recapped their adventures from the previous week. The stories about the Rabbits appeared in the first of four volumes of Milne's work at *Punch*, *The Day's Play*, in 1910.

Unbeknownst to Milne at the time, in Myra, one of the Rabbits, he created a character that was similar to the woman who would become his wife. Like Myra, Dorothy de Selincourt, had a quick wit. Daphne, as she preferred to be called, was the goddaughter of Owen Seamen. Her upbringing was full of servants and yachts and international travel, which made Ken's wife skeptical that this was the right woman for Alan. Indeed, Milne would have to work as hard as ever to make an income to keep Daphne in the lifestyle to which she was accustomed.

Milne met Daphne in January 1913 when the two were buying ski boots, coincidentally going to the same ski slopes in Switzerland. The fact that Daphne wore orange ski pants said much about her personality. Their courtship was brief. At the final Table dinner in January, Milne announced his engagement, unleashing a flood of congratulatory notes from friends and other well-wishers. Alan and Daphne were married on June 4, 1913 at St. Margaret's at Westminster Abbey with one of Ken's daughters as a bridesmaid.

They were an intriguing match. In many ways, Milne was ready to get married because he was ready to have a domestic partner to help with the things he did not want to do. He was not exactly a traditionalist when it came to gender roles, though. He and Daphne agreed that the extent of the "obey" portion of their wedding vows was her agreement to write thank you letters for him, a task that he detested. In return, Daphne was devoted to her husband's career and despite what might actually be happening, keeping up appearances that all was well.

Ken and Maud did not seem as taken with Daphne, and while Milne continued his regular visits to his brother's home for dinner, his wife rarely joined him. It is interesting to note that Christopher Milne would have much the same impression of his mother that his father had of Maria Milne. Christopher enjoyed his mother's company but did not find her particularly skilled at anything, in her case because she had not been taught to do many things. There was no need. She had servants to do things for her.

Alan and Daphne settled in a flat in Chelsea. From the start, it was Daphne's domain. If Milne wanted a say in the décor or the workings of the household, it did not matter because he was not going to get it. Still, with the optimism of a newlywed, Milne took it all in stride and used the new dimension of his life as even more semi-autobiographical writing material. He tolerated Daphne's attempts to interrupt his work while she accepted his obsession with cricket, even if she did not understand it.

Milne continued to write regularly for *Punch*, as well as the weekly paper called *Sphere,* but the signs that he was starting to burn out were there. He struggled to find fresh angles for his writing, and he grew to dread the Table dinners. Milne felt out of his element with the serious lot of gentlemen that made up the Table in 1913. It was hard to avoid talk of politics with the escalating tension in the Balkans and these discussions often left Milne agitated with his colleagues. He had always assumed that he would eventually rise to the position of editor at *Punch*, but now he questioned if he had it in him to crank out several hundred more articles over the life of his career. Could he continue to be funny for that long, that often? Given the choice, he would have preferred to write novels and plays, but he was trapped in a cycle of being forced to produce for his employer, leaving him little time for any outside writing projects. Unfortunately, the choice of what to do with his time would soon be made for him.

Chapter 5: World War I

It should come as no surprise that the young boy that could not bring himself to harm an insect would be horrified by war. Unfortunately for Milne and many other young men of the British Empire in 1914, there would be no escaping it. In the beginning, soon after the Austrian Archduke Franz Ferdinand was assassinated, it seemed that many young men looked forward to the war, or at least they looked forward to the *idea* of war. The glory, the pageantry, and the pride of fighting for their country were all that they knew at the time. No man could know the true horror that was to come in the damp, muddy, rat-infested trenches of World War I.

Milne was never one of those men who equated war with glory. He said, "War is the most babyish and laughably idiotic thing that this poor world has evolved." Still, even Milne felt compelled to contribute to the cause when war broke out. As many Europeans believed, Milne thought that winning this war against Germany would put an end to the need for future wars because, surely, democracy would prevail over German militarism. H.G. Wells published a collection of articles in 1914 called *The War that Will End War,"* and that became the ironically sad catchphrase of the conflict. It would not take long for Milne to recognize the folly in believing those words.

As work carried on at the *Punch* offices, the jokes and remarks about the men that had not yet volunteered for service grew with increasing frequency. Even though Milne had friends and colleagues who considered themselves conscientious objectors, Milne could not bring himself to do that. He did spend some time doing military drills in London and apparently became quite proficient at it. Finally, in February 1915, Milne joined the Royal Warwickshire Regiment and was commissioned as an officer in the 4th Battalion.

The difficulties he had with the abrupt transition from author and editor in charge of his own schedule to being an officer in the army was eased a bit by the fact that he already knew how to perform the drills. For a pacifist like Milne, this allowed him to contribute without actually hurting anyone, but he was the first to admit he had no idea what he was looking for when he inspected the firearms his men presented to him. He said many years later that he would hold a rifle up to the light and peer through the barrel, "and if I had seen a mouse crawling about inside I should have known something was wrong."

In the late summer of 1915, Milne was sent to Southern Command Signalling School, north of the Isle of Portland. He spent nine weeks there, training to become a signals officer. It was a good fit for Second Lieutenant Milne as it gave him some freedom over his schedule and allowed him to avoid duties he had no interest in, such as joining his battalion on marches. He was more likely to be found lecturing in a classroom on electricity. It also allowed Daphne and their servants to join him in the furnished housing provided by the British government. Milne was well aware of his good fortune considering that had he not been sent to signaling school, he would have been sent to the front lines with his old regiment, who all were killed on September 25, 1915. In the winter of 1915, Milne reported to the Isle of Wight.

War did not keep Milne from writing. His first book of essays published in the United States, *Happy Days*, received a favorable review when it came out in 1915. He also collaborated with Daphne on a play written to entertain the troops, at the request of a colonel's wife. Milne, who said he was too tired to write a play, agreed when Daphne said that he only had to dictate it, and she would do the writing. Years later, Milne fondly recalled the experience of writing with Daphne, who also performed in the play. No copies of the play exist, but it would be worked into the fairy tale, *Once on a Time,* written in 1916 when Milne was not performing his signal officer duties. Some say that this is Milne's first children's book, but he never intended it that way. In fact, he said that he wrote the book for two adults – himself and Daphne – and the satirical tale about the warring kingdoms of Euralia and Barodia is, indeed, adult fare.

Milne published remarkably little for *Punch* during his military service. It did not seem completely appropriate to him that he should write humor pieces in the midst of the war, even if he did see material all around him cloaked in the process that is the army. Certainly, there was likely little humor in his time in France on the Western Front. He received his orders to ship out to France in 1916 and found himself at the Somme Offensive. The first battle between the German Empire and the Empires of France and England lasted from July 1 and November 18. The British and French won but at a great cost. Over 600,000 of their troops were injured or killed and the casualties for both sides were well over 1,000,000 men. Milne would find much material to write about at Somme, but the rats, lice, despair, and even suicides of the men were far from humorous.

Milne took over for the senior signaling officer after he was wounded in the head by a piece of shrapnel. Part of his job was to lay telephone wire, vital to the army's communication. At one point, feeling responsible for the death of a sergeant-major who had left a trench, presumably to pass on some piece of information, Milne asked his commanding officer if he should go out and lay a line. Initially, he was told not to go but later was told to try it, but only if it was safe. Milne said later, "I promised, but felt quite unable to distinguish between common sense and cowardice. The whole thing was so damned silly."

In November 1916, Milne's time at Somme came to an end when he developed trench fever, an infectious disease passed on by body lice. When Milne's fever reached 105 degrees, he was transferred to a military hospital in Oxford. The resulting body lesions, headache, and sore joints and muscles typically required weeks of recovery time. Milne eventually did recover, but the after effects left him relegated to desk jobs for the remainder of the way. The army would get no argument from Milne, who eventually settled into a routine of working in an office in London and returning home to write plays at night.

Before he had been sent to France, Milne had written a three-act play about the age-old question of just how far people will go for money. This play explored the opportunity to earn 50,000 pounds for assuming the name Wurzel-Flummery. On his 35th birthday, Milne learned that *Wurzel-Flummery* would be produced if he could cut the three-act play to two. As difficult as it was for him to make such deep cuts to his work, the chance to have his work appear as a professional stage production won out. In April 1917, with Milne on a 48-hour leave, he and his wife went to the opening night of *Wurzel-Flummery* at New Theatre in London. The play was well received by the crowd, which had a fair share of uniformed soldiers.

Belinda was written over the course of a just a few days in October 1917, and it premiered at the New Theatre on April 8, 1918, starring British stage lend Dame Irene Vanbrugh. Ethel Barrymore played the lead role in the New York production in May, although that show's run at the Empire Theatre only lasted a month. Still, the light comedy about the flirtatious, middle-aged Belinda earned him a modest $311 in receipts from both its English and American runs. It was a goodly amount of money for the time even if it was not enough to convince Milne that he should give up his writing and editing work at *Punch* after the war.

Milne's skills as a writer were put to use in another, less known capacity during the war. When he was restricted to sedentary duty, he was assigned to Great Britain's Military Intelligence Section 7b (MI7b). This unit of the War Office was responsible for both foreign and domestic propaganda. Milne was just one of about twenty British authors who were given the responsibility of boosting the country's sagging support for the war when horror stories about life in the trenches began to spread. The authors wrote over 7,500 articles, including glowing stories of British heroism on the front lines, as well as horrific accounts of German barbarism. Press releases about the British army also filtered through MI7b.

For obvious reasons, the very existence of MI7b was kept a secret from the public. When the department was disbanded in 1918, all evidence of its existence was to be destroyed. For the most part, it was. However, Captain James Lloyd kept a stash of about 150 documents as a souvenir, as well as a pamphlet called "The Green Book." Lloyd's great-nephew made the discovery in 2013 while cleaning out Lloyd's house. Captain Lloyd had been injured in the Somme Offensive before MI7b recruited him in 1917.

"The Green Book," dated January 1919, appears to be an in-house literary pamphlet created for the amusement of the authors. They likely printed just enough copies for each of the authors in the unit and shared their satirical work at a final dinner before the department shut down. Milne expressed his distaste for his duties with MI7b with a tongue-in-cheek look at how famous writers of the past might have approached working as a propagandist. Of Captain William Shakespeare in "Some Earlier Propagandists," Milne wrote in true Shakespearean style, "In MI7b/ who loves to lie with me/ About atrocities," and "And Hun Corpse Factories/ Come hither, come hither, come hither/ Here shall we see/ No enemy/ But sit all day and blather."

Milne had assumed that once his time in the war was over, he would resume his career at *Punch*. He was ready to rejoin that comfortable and familiar life in 1919 when he inquired about being discharged from the military early. The end of the war was in sight, and he had served his time. Milne was told that if he could produce a letter from his employer attesting to how much he was needed, he could be discharged. However, it came as surprise, if not a blow to his ego, when Owen Seamen advised him that he was not, in fact, needed that much. The editor assured Milne that the magazine still wanted him to contribute his weekly article, and he would remain a member of the Table. Still, Seamen wondered, didn't Milne want to concentrate on writing his plays now? The truth was that the magazine was not particularly pleased that Milne had spent his free moments in the army working on his plays rather than writing for *Punch*. Not only that, but the elderly gentleman that had been filling in for Milne during his absence had been doing just fine.

When Milne broke the news to Daphne, she burst into tears, leaving Milne to assure her that they would not be left starving and homeless. The same week that Milne was discharged from the army he wrote his resignation letter to *Punch*. It was simply not feasible for him to survive on the payment from a single article per week. *Punch* would publish more work from Milne in the future. He would become so famous that it was the rare publication that would *not* want to feature his work. However, for all intents and purposes, Milne was sent out into the world to begin the next phase of his career, this time as a playwright.

Chapter 6: Christopher Robin is Born

On August 21, 1920, in the Milnes' apartment in Chelsea, Daphne gave birth to Christopher Robin Milne. They had been expecting a girl and they selected the name Rosemary for their child. Upon discovering they had a son, not a daughter, they had wanted to call him Billy but for reasons that are not clear, felt that William was not a suitable name for a christening. So, they opted for the name Christopher Robin and still planned to call him Billy. When Billy was old enough to talk, he called himself Billy Moon, which was as close to Billy Milne as he could come. From then on, he was Moon to family and friends. Years later, when the name Christopher Robin was so closely equated with Winnie the Pooh, Milne said that nobody in the family was fazed by it. Speaking for himself and not his son, Milne said that they were not particularly emotionally attached to the name Christopher Robin.

There would be no sibling for Billy Moon.
Daphne was far too traumatized to repeat
childbirth. She had gone into her marriage with
no understanding of sex or reproduction. Until
she was in labor with her son, she had no idea
exactly how she was going to give birth. When
she found out, she resolved that she would
never experience it again.

Milne is often cast as the child-hating children's author. It was being considered a children's author that he did not like. When Billy would write of his father being "not good" with children, it cemented the image in the public's mind of young Billy being neglected by a man who would rather be with pen and paper than his son. Truthfully, few men of the early 20th century were anything like the "involved" father of today. Billy was raised largely by nannies and governesses, as was expected at the time but that did not mean that Milne did not take an interest in his son. He wrote of him regularly to friends and family and seemed fascinated by him, even if he was not overtly affectionate or emotional about him.

Two months after Billy was born, the comedic play *The Romantic Age* opened to mixed reviews. Two more plays, *The Dover Road* and *The Truth about the Blayds,* followed in the summer of 1921 and met with greater success. Both of these plays premiered in both London and New York, earning him the considerable sum of 2,000 pounds a year. It was also that summer that Billy turned a year old. In August, Daphne went to the famous London department store, Harrods, to go shopping for a present for Christopher's first birthday. After mulling over her options, she selected a golden teddy bear that was about 18 inches high. It had movable arms and legs and an internal mechanism that made it growl. The stuffed animal was far from unique. There were hundreds like it, manufactured not far away in a factory in West London. It was named Mr. Edward, with Edward being the formal name for "Teddy." Later that year, a neighbor gave Christopher a small stuffed piglet and a stuffed donkey.

When We Were Very Young

It is quite possible that had it not been for *Wind in the Willows*, *Winnie-the-Pooh* may have never happened. Milne was firmly convinced that the 1908 Kenneth Grahame tale of personified river and woodland creatures was a classic. Grahame's inspiration came from his son, Alistair, but his grief over Alistair's suicide at the age of 19 ensured that Grahame would publish nothing after *Wind in the Willows.*

In 1921, Milne was approached about creating a dramatic adaption of Grahame's novel. There was little question that Milne would do it. He said of the book that it was the type that you gave a girl, and if she didn't like it, a young man "asks her to return his letters." Milne began working on the play right away, but it would not be until 1929 that *Toad of Toad Hall* made it to the stage in London and then, in 1930, was produced in the United States. It is the only Milne play that is still in regular production and certainly raises the question of whether or not Milne would have so eagerly agreed to do it in 1921 if he realized that the play would serve to cement his status as a children's author.

The poems that became *When We Were Very Young* did not come intentionally at first. "Vespers" was reportedly written in 1922 after Milne watched two-year old Billy kneel by his bed to say his evening prayers. It was far from sentiment that led Milne to write the poem because he was neither a Christian nor did he believe that children have any idea what they are saying when they recite prayers. More likely, it sparked an idea in him. He wrote the poem and gave it to Daphne as a gift, saying that if she liked it enough to try and get it published, she could keep the money. She sent it to *Vanity Fair*, which published "Vespers" in January 1923. Daphne pocketed $50 for her effort.

This was followed by the "Dormouse and the Doctor." Other poems, such as "Growing Up" and "Happiness" followed that and it became clear that Milne's next work was going to be a collection of children's verses. They were inspired by his own childhood, though, not of Billy's. In fact, the name "Christopher Robin" only appears in four of the poems that make up *When We Were Very Young.* Whether these verses are a true indication of Milne's childhood or whether they were more based in nostalgia is not totally clear, but these were poems taken from his own memory far more than they were an ode to Christopher Robin.

The public debut of the bear that would become Winnie the Pooh was February 13, 1924, the date *Punch* published "Teddy Bear." It was one of the poems in *When We Were Very Young,* but some of them appeared in Punch first. The first three poems of the collection that *Punch* published were not particularly visually appealing, but that problem was corrected when Ernest Shepard, *Punch's* illustrator, added the "decorations." Of the entire collection, Milne said his favorite was "Puppy and I," which was featured in an elaborate full-page spread in the magazine.

When We Were Very Young was published in London and New York in November 1924. Eight weeks later, 45,000 copies had been sold in Europe, and nearly 10,000 more copies were sold in the U.S., prompting the publisher to give Shepard a 100-pound bonus. Instead of royalties, Shepard had accepted 50 pounds up front, obviously having no idea just how popular the book would be.

By Christmas of 1925, *When We Were Very Young* was the talk of the publishing world. Critics may have been mixed on their opinions of the work, but the public was not. Milne received letters from heads of state, governors, actors, and military commanders. Word had it that President Calvin Coolidge was a fan. The public began to grow tremendously curious about Christopher Robin, to whom the book was dedicated, which would create issues in the years to come. For now, though, Milne marveled at the success at the small volume of children's poetry. He did not then nor did Milne ever consider himself to be a children's author. He tried to write an adult novel in early 1925, but the words dried up after the first chapter. Fortunately for him, the production of his plays continued. *Ariadne, To Have the Honour,* and *The Man in the Bowler Hat: A Terribly Exciting Affair* all came out around the same time as *When We Were Young.* With *Portrait of a Gentleman in Slippers,*" they would form the book *Four Plays* in 1926.

Milne's success with the new book of children's verses and the productions of his plays came just as things were taking a turn for the worse for his brother. Ken was diagnosed with tuberculosis in 1924. This forced him to give up his job as a civil servant, but Milne tried to put a positive spin on it. He told Ken that now he had no choice but to focus on his writing, not because he needed to financially but because, at 43, he was much too young to retire and do nothing. Milne insisted that he be allowed to contribute to an education fund for Ken's children and other financial needs that they may have. Milne was careful to tread lightly, not wanting to make Ken feel as if whatever his brother offered was too much to accept. However, Ken must have realized that he did need his brother's help. Most of the time, he was relegated to a chair in the country, away from the smoggy city air. Meanwhile, Alan Milne was about to go from being a successful playwright and author to one of the biggest stars in the literary world.

Winnie the Pooh (1926 to 28)

While Winnie the Pooh did not exist yet in 1925, a bear named Winnie did. Winnie was short for Winnipeg, the city in Ontario, Canada. She was motherless American Black Bear cub when Lieutenant Harry Colebourn of the Canadian Cavalry purchased her. He raised the cub in his hometown of Winnipeg before she eventually made her way to the London Zoo in 1915, which was her home until her death in 1934.

Billy liked to visit the London Zoo, and he was quite taken with Winnie, as were many of the children that visited the zoo. He had decided that Edward Bear, by now his constant companion, was in need of a new name. Milne said that one day when Billy was about five years old, they were leaving the zoo and Billy announced that his bear was now named Winnie. Milne asked if he had given his bear a girl's name and Billy corrected himself, saying that his bear was Winnie the Pooh, which in his mind was a boy's name. Young Billy Moon had borrowed the name Pooh from a swan.

In light of the success of *When We Were Very Young*, Milne received pressure to follow it up with another children's book. He did contribute stories to paintings from American painter H. Willebeek Le Mair. What he did not count on was the star power of his name and in a rather unwise business decision, he agreed to a lump sum payment of 200 pounds rather than asking for royalties. The move cost him thousands of pounds, but he felt better after he was paid handsomely for merely signing 500 copies of *A Gallery of Children*, his collection of 12 children's short stories.

It was around Christmas 1925 that Milne sat down to try to think of a children's story for the Christmas edition of the *Evening News.* After some struggling, he took Daphne's suggestion and reworked a bedtime story that he had told Billy, or more accurately, wrote something around the idea of the story. What he wrote was the story of Winnie the Pooh being dragged down the stairs by Christopher Robin, hitting his head along each step, thinking that he would like the bumping to stop but believing it was the only way down the stairs. It would become the first chapter of *Winnie-the-Pooh*.

On Christmas Eve, rather than printing a news headline, the *Evening News* printed a banner headline announcing that "A Children's Story by A.A. Milne" appeared on Page 7 and would be broadcast on all London radio stations the following evening at 7:45 p.m. as part of the children's Christmas programming. The story promised to be about Christopher Robin and his teddy bear. When readers turned to Page 7 of the paper, they were greeted with the words "Winnie-the-Pooh" in giant letters.

At the request of his son and wife, Milne wrote a book devoted to Winnie the Pooh. Already with Piglet and Eeyore, he invented the characters of Owl and Rabbit but felt as if he needed more. He and Daphne made a return trip to Harrods with the expressed purpose of finding new characters for his book. Stuffed kangaroos fit the bill and Kanga – the only female character in the story – and Roo were born. Unfortunately, the toy Roo was later lost in the woods and never found.

Winnie-the-Pooh was complete by March 1926. This was not the only project on Milne's plate, though. A new book of verses, which would become *Now We Are Six*, was in the works. He was also working on a slim volume of four short stories called *The Secret*, which was released in limited edition in 1929. Milne was also wrapping up the final proofs of *Four Plays,* which was published on April 15. In all, it was a hugely manageable to-do list for Milne, which gave him time to focus on the production of *Winnie-the-Pooh.* He had a say in nearly every piece of the book's creation, including the illustration, layout, and design. Having an illustrator contribute to a book was not typical for the time but was crucial to *Winnie-The-Pooh*. However, even though Shepard created them he never owned them. He and Milne worked out a separate arrangement in which Milne would pay him a share of his own royalties. They kept that arrangement for the two books that would follow. When licensing rights were sold for the likeness of Pooh and the other characters, Shepard was not involved.

Milne was remarkably specific with Shepard about how he wanted the characters to appear. Given that the artist was trying to create drawings from ideas created in Milne's mind, Milne thought it would be helpful if he saw the toys in Billy's nursery. Even seeing the toys did not give Shepard the exact dimensions that Milne wanted for the characters, especially for Piglet. The stuffed Piglet was nearly the same size as Pooh, but for the sake of the stories, it was important that he be very small. Shepard resisted using Billy's toys as models, though. His own son had a teddy bear, and he said he used that for his model instead. In fact, he claimed that used his son as the model for Christopher Robin, but even Christopher Milne agreed that the drawings of Christopher Robin bear a strong resemblance to him as a boy, right down to the sturdy legs and the shaggy hair.

Shepard did visit Milne's Cotchford Farm in Ashdown Forest. Milne purchased it as a weekend retreat for his family in 1924. The old farmhouse, which dated back to at least the 16th century, was not in good shape when Milne bought it. It would not be usable until the spring of 1925, but once it was ready, Milne loved it. In Christopher Milne's biography, he wrote that for anyone who read the Pooh books, they would have a very clear idea of what Ashdown Forest was like because Pooh's Forest and Ashdown Forest were one in the same. Milne's country home gave him a singularly real setting for his characters. Even if the characters were personified versions of his son's toys, where they lived was real.

The reason that trees are such a dominant symbol in the Pooh books is that Billy spent so much time in trees. He loved to climb trees, undaunted even if he fell from one. Of course, the fictional Christopher Robin never tumbled out of a tree nor really made any sort of mistake. He seemed to be quite wise and resourceful for a boy of six years old, always there to keep Pooh and friends from harm's way, or at least long-term harm. It is his seemingly perfect childhood that put off many readers. It is likely that many Pooh fans would have been happy to simply read about Pooh and his friends and not have Christopher Robin interrupt the story. It is no accident on Milne's part that he made Christopher Robin this way. In these stories, Christopher Robin is the adult and the toys are the children. In the eyes of many children, adults do not make mistakes like fall out of trees.

There was a bit of a bidding war for the manuscripts as *Winnie-the-Pooh* neared publication. Milne had made the mistake of selling the manuscript of *When We Were Young*, of course having no idea how valuable it would be. He did not want to make the same mistake with *Winnie-the-Pooh*. So, instead of trying to guess what a fair price would be, he opted not to sell at all. Per his instructions in his will, the manuscripts to *Winnie-the-Pooh* and *The House on Pooh Corner* are the property of his alma mater, Trinity College at the University of Cambridge.

Winnie-the-Pooh was published to much fanfare in London and New York in October 1926. Sales did not disappoint. The initial 32,000 copies that were printed were snapped up by eager fans. It was as well received as *When We Were Very Young*, with some saying that it was even better. It no doubt pleased Milne that some of the adult readers recognized that this was a story of reflection on a simpler time, his childhood, and it was his ability to capture the adults readers that helped drive the book toward literary immortality.

With his growing fame came the honor of being invited to join the Athenaeum Club in London. Named for Athens when it was considered the seat of cultural refinement, the Athenaeum was an exclusive membership of intellectuals who had attained some sort of outstanding achievement in science, the arts, or literature. Election required unanimous approval by the selection committee and Milne was rightfully proud of his selection. However, none of the fame or the money that was now flowing in at a regular pace led to a sudden desire for a larger home or a fleet of cars. Milne knew that he had not only his son's future to save for, but he had taken on financial responsibility for Ken, and he made sure that he took those responsibilities into account. That did not mean he was stingy – far from it. He did not hesitate to spend money on what he liked, which included nice clothes, fine wine, tickets to cricket matches, and his fair share of golf equipment. Daphne also wanted for nothing.

Milne was prepared for all of the attention that *Winnie-the-Pooh* would bring. He wrote it with a sequel in mind and the ending of *Winnie-the-Pooh* left the door open for more to come. Milne had already written several of the 35 verses that appear in *Now We Are Six* before *Winnie-the-Pooh* hit the bookstores. Shepard also illustrated *Now We Are Six*, published in October 1927, and 11 of the poems feature illustrations of Pooh. As *Now We Are Six* was in the production process, Milne started to work on the second Pooh book. He was anxious to see how Shepard would portray his new character. "I'm longing to see the Tigger illustrations," he wrote to him.

British critics were not as impressed with *Now We Are Six* as the American critics were although Milne had set the bar so high that anything he produced after that was bound to pale in comparison. However, Pooh and friends had developed such as fan base by this time that it did not matter what critics said. Copies of the book flew off the shelves and the sales of *When We Were Very Young,* and *Winnie-the-Pooh* continued to climb. With the success of his play *The Ivory Door,* which was enjoyed a decent run in New York, 1927 was a very good year for the Milne family, despite Billy Moon's bout with the chicken pox in December.

The final Winnie the Pooh book, *The House at Pooh Corner,* was published in October 1928. Milne had already announced that this would be it for Pooh. His reasons had as much to do with giving his son his name back as they did with wanting to move away, once and for all, from his label as a children's author. Billy was growing up and entering the world of prep school and soccer. Gone was the boyish haircut that so many readers recognized from Shepard's drawings. Milne was aware that the line he had drawn between the real Christopher Robin and the Christopher Robin of fiction was growing ever more fuzzy. He did not like this because he had been terribly clear with himself from the beginning that the boy he wrote about in the Pooh books was fiction. Now, he was not so sure, and he did not want his son to lose his identity to a fictional character. He wrote, "I do not want C.R. Milne to ever wish that his names were Charles Robert."

There was also the matter of being able to continue the success of the Pooh character. Milne was not sure that he could do it. It did not seem possible that he could keep thinking of stories about Pooh and Christopher Robin that were good enough for people to continue to want to read. No doubt, people would buy the books because they had grown attached to the characters, but for Milne, it seemed safer to get out while he was still on top. However, he was sadly mistaken if he thought he could ever be thought of anything but the creator of Winnie the Pooh.

Chapter 7: Milne's Later Career

Milne had wanted to believe that his brother, Barry, had been exaggerating Ken's condition. Perhaps it was because Ken had been living with tuberculosis for so long that the fact that Ken had become bedridden was not particularly alarming. He had recovered before, he could recover again. Milne wrote to J.V. in the spring of 1929 that he was planning a trip to see Ken to check on his condition for himself. Sadly, it was as bad as Barry made it out to be and Ken died at the age of 48 on May 21 of that year. A grief-stricken Alan Milne could not bring himself to sit through the service in the church, but he hovered in the churchyard, alone with his thoughts. When Milne wrote his autobiography years later, it was dedicated to Ken. He maintained a close relationship with Maud as he did with Barry's wife, Connie. His good fortune in his career allowed him to see to it that Maud was financially comfortable for the rest of her life.

It was obviously not finances that pushed Milne to make an intriguing decision about the rights to the image of Winnie the Pooh. Starting in 1930, the Winnie the Pooh image belonged to Stephen Slesinger, creator of numerous well-known brands and trademarks for characters taken from cartoons or the pages of children's books. Today, most people know Winnie the Pooh as the tubby gold bear with a red shirt. Shepard did not draw him that way. That was the work of Slesinger. For reasons that are not entirely known, Milne sold his rights to the Pooh image to Slesinger for 3 percent of the total sales and anywhere between 15 to 50 percent of certain products capitalizing on the Winnie the Pooh brand, which includes the likenesses of Eeyore, Tigger, Owl, Piglet, and Christopher Robin. Who knows why Milne did it. Perhaps it was his way of trying to be rid of making decisions about Winnie the Pooh. Doubtful that he knew just how lucrative the Winnie the Pooh brand would become.

As his career moved on post- Winnie the Pooh, Milne tried to face the labels slapped on him head-on. He wrote in the preface of the play *The Ivory Door*, "I have the Whimsical label so firmly round my own neck that I can neither escape from it or focus it." He confessed that he suspected that, no matter what he wrote, he would be accused of being whimsical or steeped in fantasy. With that, he presented *The Ivory Door* as the best play he had written to date, virtually assuring that critics would go out of their way to prove him wrong.

The Ivory Door had a very brief run in London. It was more successful in New York despite the *New Yorker* declaring that the play had a "lethal combination of whimsy and lethargy." While Milne lamented the harsh reviews plays often receive on opening night, something that he viewed as unfair judgment, he suggested that maybe he would be better off without the theatre. He did not mean it, of course. He still had another hit play in him.

He began working on *Michael and Mary* in the summer of 1929. There was not much that could be described as whimsical about this play. The plot involves the illegal marriage of a couple after the wife is abandoned by her first husband. The first husband eventually turns up and begins to blackmail Michael and Mary, who got married for the sake of the child they had together. The play ends with their son forgiving them and kissing their joined hands, a move that made many Brits uncomfortable for its display of a man kissing another man, even if it was intended to be a son kissing his father.

Perhaps it was questions about his own marriage, which would change as his career would no longer be the family's focal point, which kept marriage at the forefront of his creative mind. After *Michael and Mary*, he began to work on the novel *Two People.* The story of Reginald and Sylvia Wellard is told from Reginald's point of view. He is a writer, which allows Milne to get in some jabs about the theatre industry when Reginald's novel is made into a play. The couple seems to have remarkably little in common other than the fact they love each other. Sylvia contributes little in the way of intellectual stimulation but is quite good at adoring her husband.

There is much to suggest that this was a glimpse into Alan and Daphne's marriage. That fate that all writers dread, the lack of new material, began to plague Milne in the early 1930s. The public was quite clear on what it wanted from Milne, but he was not going to provide it. He lamented the fact that, in his eyes, all of his articles, essays, poems, plays, and novels were wiped away by the 70,000 words he wrote about the make-believe world of his son's stuffed toys. The success of his adaptation of *The Wind in the Willows* did not help his cause. The play was a terrific success and Milne watched with pleasure when Kenneth Grahame and his wife attended an early performance with smiles on their faces. Milne admired Grahame for his ability to allow his characters and words to be altered by another author, something he was not sure that he could do himself. Of course, the connection between the Wild Wood of *The Wind in the Willows* and Winnie the Pooh's Forest was an easy leap to make. Many believed that it was obvious that Milne understood children's characters, even if he eventually believed that to be a curse more than a blessing.

Unfortunately, it was not as if he was brimming with ideas for new stories. He wasn't, and as he became less in demand, Daphne became more bored. She had grown accustomed to the steady stream of attention that her husband had commanded. When that began to decline, she looked elsewhere for excitement. The Milnes never divorced, and Alan seemed intent on presenting them as a united front, even when Daphne was away. Their first trip to New York in 1931 was the only time that Alan visited the U.S., but it was just the beginning of regular excursions to the U.S. for Daphne.

When they first arrived, with Christopher remaining behind at boarding school, Milne was pleased that the customs officer recognized his name. That changed to slight irritation as it seemed that all he was known for in the U.S. was Winnie the Pooh. He was inundated for requests for interviews, and many were curious about Christopher Robin. What was he up to now? Would there be a sequel with Christopher Robin all grown up? What was it like to "Christopher Robin's father?" Milne did take the opportunity to show photos of his son and brag about Christopher's cricket prowess. He assured reporters that his most important work in progress was helping the real Christopher Robin develop as a person. Daphne fielded questions about her son, too, and noted that she saw a big difference between English children and American children. It seemed to her that American children were much more grown up and mature because they had earlier entry into the adult world, while English children were kept in a distinct and separate world from adults for a longer period of time.

The official reason for the trip was to see the opening of his new play, *They Don't Mean Any Harm*, as well as to promote *Two People.* The promotional tour must have worked because the book wound up a bestseller in the U.S. The Milnes enjoyed New York and Daphne remarked that is was much more beautiful than she was expecting. They also could not help but notice the effects of the Great Depression, as it was 1931. The beauty of Central Park was juxtaposed with men, some dressed in suits that used to be part of their office wardrobe, in long and winding lines at soup kitchens.

It as on the first trip to New York that the Milnes saw the American playwright Elmer Rice. They knew him from his trip to London the previous year after he won the Pulitzer Prize for his play, *Street Scene.* Milne liked Rice, but Daphne was especially taken by him. She would return to New York many times in the 1930s and would spend much of her time with Rice. Based on Rice's writing about the folly of monogamy and Daphne's hurt feelings years later when he lost interest in her, there is evidence to suggest that Rice and Daphne carried on a lengthy affair, which was the reason for her frequent trips to the U.S. Milne was aware of who she was with, but if he knew anything more, he did not let on. He did not try to hide her absences and seemed to accept their increasing separations as a natural evolution in their relationship.

However, this does not mean that Milne was spending his time back in London alone. He was frequently seen around town with the actress Leonora Corbett, who had preformed in a revival of Milne's *Belinda*. They were obviously supremely comfortable with each other, and she seemed to be the stand-in for Daphne when she was in New York. Some said that the "affair" between Milne and Corbett was well known. In fact, she was also known to Maud as Milne continued his close relationship with Ken's wife and children.

The same could not be said for his relationship with Barry. Despite Alan's urging, Milne's father changed his will so that Barry and not his wife Connie would receive the bulk of J.V's estate. Alan did not want Barry, a lawyer, even associated with the writing of the will, let alone having control of the money. He told J.V. that if his intent was to ensure that Connie was cared for he needed to leave the money directly to her but J.V. did not listen After J.V. died on June 11, 1932, Milne never spoke to his brother again. Not even Barry's attempts to reconcile when he was dying of throat cancer would move Milne to see him again.

As for Christopher, now having outgrown the name Billy but still "Moon" to his father, he seemed to serve as a replacement for Ken. As an adult, Christopher harbored some bitterness about this as he did about nearly everything in his childhood. He claimed that it allowed his father to stay a child. At the time, though, Christopher was devoted to his father and appreciated the talks and walks and the games they played together. His anxiety about being "Christopher Robin" was just beginning to take shape and showed itself in his tendency to get tongue-tied and overwhelmed when he tried to speak. He also harbored doubts that he could ever meet the expectations that he believed his father had set for him.

In the five years that followed J.V.'s death, Milne published six books. One was his autobiography, titled *It's Too Late Now* but marketed as a magazine serial in the *Atlantic Monthly,* and simply as *Autobiography* in the U.S. Apparently, Americans thought the actual title was too gloomy. It was published in September 1939, and it sold well, despite the world's preoccupation with events in Germany. Milne had agreed to a lower advance in anticipation that war might interrupt sales but that was not the case. In fact, as his other books continued to sell, his publisher had difficulty finding enough paper for printing due to paper shortages.

If his fans were hoping for glimpse into the life of Christopher Robin's father during the Winnie the Pooh years, they were disappointed in his autobiography. Much of the book was spent where Milne always seemed he would rather be – his own childhood. Only a few pages were devoted to the years that his son was growing up, and Winnie the Pooh was taking the world by storm. Even though the book is dedicated to Ken, there is no mention at all of Ken's death. Grief was too private for Milne to share in print.

None of the books were met with any particular acclaim, although one, *Peace with Honour*, did cause quite a stir as England was on the verge of war with Germany. Milne had maintained his position as a pacifist for years, a position strengthened, not weakened by his service in World War I. *Peace With* Honor, which was published in September 1934, was his plea for the world to avoid war. It sold well upon its release and nearly matched the other hot nonfiction seller of the time, the autobiography of his friend, H.G. Wells.

Milne's case against war was met with mixed reaction, though. He received letters of admiration from some, including the former Queen of Romania. Requests for him to speak publicly against the war were declined, though, as Milne never prided himself as an accomplished public speaker. Others saw Milne as incredibly naïve about war and his refusal to accept the idea that some wars are, in fact, just. One such critic was the American author T.S. Eliot. In January 1935, Eliot wrote an essay for *Time and Tide* in which he criticized Milne for not recognizing that there are some things worse than war.

Eliot's essay was harsh although many would come to agree that Eliot was right. Even Milne would eventually make an exception to his point of view. In his defense, he had no way of knowing what a maniacal dictator Adolf Hitler had come to be. With London itself under direct attack and democracy in danger of being overwhelmed by Hitler's Nazi regime, Milne relented. Indeed, war had come directly to his doorstep in more ways than one. By 1940, he was now living exclusively at Cotchford and part of the farm was taken over by the British government as a camp for evacuees. Rather than fuss with the lengthy forms required by the government, he simply donated his land to the cause. Milne came to know some of the people who lived in the field were the family's donkey used to roam. When the evacuees were returned to London, Milne even wrote a poem about them and how they were remarkably more easy to please than any other guest he had hosted at his farm.

Christopher was a student at Cambridge, having won a scholarship far more lucrative than his father's, when war broke out. Like most young men, he joined the army when war was declared, and he was eventually assigned to the Royal Engineers. Christopher said that it took his years in the war for him to finally find his authentic self, separate from the boy that his father had created on paper. He considered his military service as the foundation of his adulthood. Meanwhile, Milne followed his son's progress and with worry and anxiety. His anxiety was further heightened by the telegram from the British War Office on October 7, 1944. Christopher had been wounded in Italy while serving as a platoon commander. No other information was provided, other than the wound was "serious." However, it turned out that the wound was not that serious and required a minor operation to remove pieces of broken bone from his head. Christopher wrote to his father that he found the whole experience to be "interesting." His proud father said that while his son had inherited much from him, the notion that being wounded in combat was an enthralling experience was not one of them.

In 1941, Milne had begun work on his first novel in over a decade, *Chloe Marr*. Chloe is a thoroughly modern single woman of the 40s with her share of male admirers but a woman who seemed incapable of loving any of them. This is adult fare but given the light, Milne touch. Some reviewers could not help but use the word whimsical but overall, reviewers gave it credit for the adult novel that it is. The reviews were generally positive, and it sold well when it was finally published after the war in 1946, but it was the last novel that Milne would write.

Milne's continued to write for adults, mostly short stories, but they did not sell. His American publisher had tried to push forward a big promotion of his adult literature, but the interest was simply not there. Nearly a quarter million of his books were sold a discount prices simply to clear the shelf space. This was far from the case for his children's books. In 1947, Christopher's toys made their own tour of the United States, complete with birth certificates that were handwritten by A.A. Milne. An indication of the value of the inspiration for the Pooh stories was the insurance policy that was taken out on them once they arrived in New York. They were insured for the $50,000, which was an enormous sum at the time. The toys made their way across the U.S. for years, stopping at bookstores, department stores, and libraries, much to the delight of the legion of Pooh's fans. Christopher said he had no hard feelings about his toys eventually finding a permanent home at the New York Public Library, as they were a part of his past. His father's only stipulation was that they never be cleaned, wanting them to always look as if Billy Moon had just returned them to the shelf.

Chapter 8: Milne's Death and Legacy

Milne's relationship with his son began to deteriorate after Christopher returned from the war. Milne's biographer, Ann Thwaite, notes that Christopher did not have a true adolescence as a child. So, he went through his rebellious period as an adult. He remained convinced for the rest of his life that his father exploited his childhood for profit. As many children of celebrities discover, paving his own path was not easy. Certainly his attempts to be a writer were going to draw comparisons, and when that happened, this only served to fuel his bitterness.

Neither Daphne nor Alan approved of Christopher's wife. Lesley de Selincourt was Christopher's first cousin, the daughter of Daphne's brother, Aubrey. Daphne had not spoken to Aubrey for 25 years, since he borrowed money that he never repaid. That alone was problematic but the fact that the young couple was so closely related caused further concerns. No doubt eyebrows were raised, and there were whispers behind closed doors when Christopher and Lesley's only child, a daughter, was born severely disabled. Nonetheless, they were married on July 24, 1948.

If Christopher's marriage hurt his relationship with his parents, it did seem to help draw Alan and Daphne closer. They had already begin to drift back together, and their concern for their son further united them. Meanwhile, Christopher solidified the rift between himself and his parents by moving with his wife to a town that was 200 miles away to manage a bookstore. Daphne told Christopher that she found it odd that he would choose to operate a bookstore, which would only leave him to face daily questions about his father and Winnie the Pooh.

Milne's final book was published in 1952 when he was 70 years old. *Year In, Year Out* was a series of essays on Milne's take on the world. It received positive reviews, overall, and sold well. Maybe it was age, or maybe it was nostalgia, but a letter to young fan, a budding writer like Milne once was, showed that Milne's bitterness toward his legacy was softening. He thanked the young man for his kind words about both *Winnie-the-Pooh* and his latest work and said that now a "nice comfortable feeling" came over him when he thought of Pooh. An autobiographical poem that he wrote for the *New York Herald* when *Year In, Year Out* was published in the U.S. later that year contained the lines,

> This so happy an adventure is
> Coming (so I must suppose
> Now I'm 70) to a close.
> Take it all, year in, year out
> I've enjoyed it
> Not a doubt.

On October 15, Milne suffered a stroke and was taken by ambulance to East Grinstead Hospital in London. Daphne was told he had only days to live but, in fact, he lived another three years. They were not fruitful or happy ones. He chose to have brain surgery in December that was promised to cure him or kill him, but it did neither. It only left him partially paralyzed and with a more disagreeable, vulgar personality that was unrecognizable to his friends and family. He spent most of the final years and months of his life confined to a wheelchair, although he did occasionally find the strength to write a bit. His last public writing was a letter to the *Times* in 1954 on the subject of subsidiary rights and booksellers.

Alan Milne died on January 31, 1956 at the age of 74. His memorial service was held at All-Hallows-by-the Tower in London and included a reciting of "Vespers," the poem he had written for Daphne after watching Christopher say his prayers. Christopher did attend the service, although his pregnant wife did not. Daphne was horrified that he wore a shabby overcoat to the service, and no doubt she told him so. It was the last time she saw her son, even though she lived another 15 years. She had her sculpture of Christopher buried in the yard so she would never have to see it again. Christopher would go on to write his own version of his life events in *Enchanted Places* and *The Path Through The Trees.* He decided against asking anyone to help by providing his or her own memories of his father and his childhood. That way, he said, nobody could tell him that he got it wrong. Christopher Robin Milne died in April 20, 1996 after a lengthy illness.

Chapter 9: Winnie-the-Pooh Lives On

Even though it may not have been what he wanted, the legacy of Alan Milne is thoroughly and solely wrapped up in Winnie the Pooh. It was a bittersweet legacy for Milne. It cost him his relationship with his son, but it was the success of his children's books that gave him the financial security to write what he wanted, something that he longed to do in the early days of his career when he struggled to piece together a living as a freelancer. The problem was that readers did not want to read what he wanted to write. They wanted Winnie the Pooh and Milne's death did nothing to slow down demand.

The rights to Winnie the Pooh and the associated characters were sold to Walt Disney Productions in 1961. Being part of the Disney machine has ensured that the popularity of Winnie the Pooh goes far beyond the two Pooh novels, which a significant number of people claiming to be Pooh fans have never read. In today's world, children are introduced to Pooh through DVDs, t-shirts, cups, hats, and any number of toys and other products licensed by Disney. The sales of Pooh related products rakes in over $3 billion a year for Disney, making Winnie the Pooh second only to Mickey Mouse as the most marketable children's character. For the traditionalists, *Winnie-the-Pooh* is still in print, a remarkable feat for a children's book published in 1925. It has been translated into 46 languages since its initial publication in 1926.

Christopher's well-worn stuffed animals continue to be the property of the New York Public Library, where they have sat in a bulletproof case since 1987. Visitors trek to the library from around the world to get a glimpse at the "original" Pooh and library personnel report that the toys have been witness to numerous wedding proposals. Some visitors simply break into tears at the site of the inspiration for the characters that meant so much to them as children.

One has to wonder what Milne would have thought about another author carrying on the Pooh series, but that is what happened in 2009, 81 years after the publication of *The House on Pooh Corner.* The Trustees of Pooh Properties wanted to see it happen but would only entrust such a project to the right author. After some searching, the project was awarded to English author and director David Benedictus. He had already written and produced audio recordings of Winnie the Pooh stories and wanted to pick up where *The House on Pooh Corner* left off. Benedictus wrote two sample stories and sent them to the trustees and waited. And waited. Finally, after ten years, he received a reply. He had been selected to carry on the tales of Pooh and friends.

Predictably, the idea of Benedictus entering such sacred ground drew cries of horror from many in the literary community. Many wondered why it was necessary to attempt such a feat and worried about what would happen if Benedictus failed. Would a flop of a sequel scare children away from the original stories? Michael Brown, the chairman of Pooh Properties, disagreed. He said that the new book would simply continue the stories that Milne began without doing any damage to the first Pooh books.

Another argument against the sequel is that there is already so much Winnie the Pooh merchandise that it would be difficult for a new book to stand out as anything significant. However, this issue is beyond the scope of Pooh Properties. The plethora of movies, television shows, and video games featuring Winnie the Pooh belong to Disney.

Return to the Hundred Acre Wood, a collection of ten new Pooh stories, was released in October 2009. To further fuel the controversy, Benedictus introduced a new character, Lottie the Otter. He described her as "a bit of a snob." His first idea for a new character, a green snake, was not warmly received. Some said that a snake was far too scary for a Pooh story. With a project like this, Benedictus had to accept a great deal of input from a variety of interested parties, something that he normally does not accept easily. He did take a subtle shot at Disney when he said that the corporation would be inviting a lawsuit if he hears of any of the Disney films featuring an otter.

However, Benedictus said that he tried very hard to be as faithful to Milne as he could. To that end, he visited Ashdown Forest and read everything by Milne that he could get his hands on. Then, Benedictus said, "I felt I could become him." He was careful to stay as true to the characters as he could. Not much changed in Hundred Acre Wood under Benedictus's watch. Pooh, Tigger, Eeyore, and the gang are the same as when Milne put down his pen. The only one who changed at all is Christopher Robin, who is back from boarding school. According to Benedictus, keeping Milne's world unchanged was notable because Milne specifically created an unchanging world. The danger was in creating a parody.

Bookstores around the U.S. heralded the news of the arrival of a new Pooh book with tea parties and "poohtiques." Penguin Books commissioned a permanent mural for the New York Public Library's Children Center, featuring a map of Hundred Acre Wood. The map was a reproduction of the one drawn by E.H. Shepard and not the new Winnie the Pooh illustrator, Mark Burgess. Reviews about the book were mixed. Some critics said that Benedictus made the book too much like an imitation of Milne. Others said it was charming and a pleasant return to a familiar place.

One of the more intriguing uses of the Winnie the Pooh characters has been Benjamin Hoff's 1982 book, *The Tao of Pooh*. The book, which was a bestseller in the U.S., used Milne's characters to try to explain the principles of Taoism. Ten years later, Hoff followed it up with *The Te of Piglet*. Is using Winnie the Pooh as an example of the concept of effortless doing taking the character that began life as a stuffed bear from Harrods taking Milne's idea too far? If so, digging into the psychology and philosophy of Pooh has been difficult for some people to resist.

There have been many attempts to analyze Winnie the Pooh. Essays that take a critical approach to the world that Milne created offer theories on why there is only one female character in the story. Others expound on why Eeyore is so gloomy and Tigger is so reckless while in the back of their minds, they think the characters remind them of people they know. Some argue that the stories offer unhealthy lessons on escapism and lack of responsibility, although Milne might respond today that escapism and lack of responsibility was entirely the point of the stories.

Milne created what was at the same time a remarkably safe world free from war or natural disasters. No modern technology such as telephones or automobiles invaded Pooh's Forest. Many days are spent eating and exploring. There is something very appealing to that to many adults, who can be credited with keeping the Pooh legacy alive. It is the adults who fondly look back on their own initial introduction to Winnie the Pooh and want their children to have that experience, too. Similar to the parents who revisit *Wind in the Willows*, it is only as adults that the true genius of Milne's creation is revealed. Much of the humor is far too sophisticated for most children to grasp, but it presents a delightful surprise to the parent who suddenly "gets" what went right over his head decades before. With that comes the revelation that maybe Milne was right all along, and he was much more than an author of children's literature. He was an author for everyone.

References

Blundell, Nigel and Emily Hill. "Happy 90th
Birthday, Winnie the Pooh." *The Daily Mail.* June
11, 2001.
http://www.dailymail.co.uk/news/article-
2002613/Winnie-Pooh-The-bear-little-brain-
VERY-big-bank-balance.html

Ensor, Josie. "Agony of A.A. Milne, Reluctant
Wartime Propagandist, and the 'lies' about
German atrocities." *The Telegraph.* April 24,
2013. http://www.telegraph.co.uk/history/britain-
at-war/10015206/Agony-of-AA-Milne-the-
reluctant-wartime-propagandist-and-the-lies-
about-German-atrocities.html

Flood, Alison. "Winnie-the-Pooh Author A.A. Milne was First World War Propagandist." *The Guardian.* April 26, 2013. http://www.theguardian.com/books/2013/apr/26/milne-first-world-war-propaganda

Leonard, Devin and Doris Burke. "The Curse of Pooh." *Fortune.* January 20, 2003. http://money.cnn.com/magazines/fortune/fortune_archive/2003/01/20/335653/

"History of Punch." *Punch.* http://www.punch.co.uk

Lee, Felicia R. "The Same Pooh Bear, But an Otter Has Arrived." *The New York Times.* October 4, 2009. http://www.nytimes.com/2009/10/05/books/05pooh.html?_r=0

Milne, Christopher. *The Enchanted Places.* London: Methuen Publishing Ltd. 1974.

Neary, Lynn. "Pooh Faithful Return to Hundred Acre Wood." NPR. October 2, 2009. http://www.npr.org/2009/10/02/113406207/pooh-faithful-return-to-the-hundred-acre-wood

Thwaite, Ann. *A.A. Milne: The Man Behind Winnie-the-Pooh.* New York: Random House. 1990.

CPSIA information can be obtained
at www.ICGtesting.com
Printed in the USA
LVOW07s1629161017
552619LV00041B/2119/P

9 781494 771812